Knowledge
Is
Power

Navigating the Real Estate Financing Process

JONATHAN L. WOODS

ISBN-10: 1983938432
ISBN-13: 978-1983938436

DEDICATION

This book is dedicated to my best friend, confidant and love of my life:
Dianne

CONTENTS

ACKNOWLEDGMENTS

This book is meant to be a starting point for anyone wishing to arm themselves with information regarding the Real Estate financing process. I have attempted to include in these pages some of the issues and "pitfalls" that I have seen in my 25-year career that have caused anxiety and anxiousness for everyone involved in the mortgage process.

Mortgage financing is a stressful process as it is. It is my hope that by reading this text, you will be able to make an informed decision as to the best route for you to take in your home financing decision. Happy reading!

What Could Possibly Go Wrong?

If you applied for a mortgage 20 years ago, you likely heard "press hard, there are three copies" when completing your initial loan application paperwork. In recent years, the mortgage loan process has become more standardized, computerized and can realistically be completed in under 30 days. But even in that seemingly short timeframe, things still can and do go wrong. Here are a few of them that I have seen.

I'm mad as hell and I'm not going to take it anymore!

Even if your new boss doesn't share the rest of the company's amazing opinion of you, walking out of your 4-year career with the company while you are in the middle of the mortgage process just doesn't make good sense. Sure, you may be able to quickly land in a new (maybe even better) position at another firm, but your loan file will basically be "on hold" until you get there.

Once you DO land your new job, you will need to actually get a paycheck (which typically takes 2-3 weeks) and provide a copy of it to your mortgage team. From there, they will need to make sure that the new position, income and debt ratios can be approved by their credit people. Since the entire mortgage process today should basically take 30 days or less, my advice to you is to bite your tongue and wait until after you've closed on your mortgage before you make any long-term decisions here. The short-term pain can seem severe, but if you are in the middle of purchasing your dream home, you could be creating even greater pain for yourself.

I've worked hard for my money and I deserve a new car.

Yes, you have worked hard for your money. And yes, you may truly deserve a new car. The issue is not whether or not you have earned the right to purchase a new car. The issue is how tight are your qualifying ratios for your new home loan?

If you are like many Americans, you likely have several credit cards, a couple of car loans and maybe even some student loan debt already. These things are all considered by the credit team when determining if you have the ability to repay your new mortgage. If your qualifying ratios are close, you might have just kicked yourself out of your new home by buying that new car.

On the other hand, if you are a person who rarely uses debt to finance large purchases like new cars, then as long as you are being reasonable in your new home expectations, you likely won't be hurt by this type of purchase in the long term. You will, however, cost yourself some additional time because the paperwork for the new car loan will have to be copied and sent to the mortgage team so that they can make sure you still have the ability to pay for your new mortgage.

What do you mean "The appraisal came in low"?

Sometimes, especially in an active real estate market, home prices increase at a rapid pace. Generally speaking, this means that there are fewer homes on the market than potential buyers would like and creates what is called a "Seller's Market". In these instances, sellers and Realtors will do their best to estimate what the current value of a home for sale is, but for obvious reasons, both of these parties would like to sell the home for as much as humanly possible. For the seller, they would be able to net more from the sale of the home and for the Realtor, their commission would be higher since it would be calculated on a higher sales price.

The problem in these types of markets comes when the mortgage team sends out an independent third party (a real estate Appraiser) to give an objective opinion of the current market value of the home being sold. If the current (meaning before today, but within the past 6 months) sales of "comparable" homes within a short distance from your new home have all sold for less than you are paying, there may be an issue with value. You can still pay the agreed-upon price for the home, but your mortgage team can only lend based on the LESSER of the sales price or the appraised value. This means that if you choose to go ahead at the higher price, you will be responsible for paying the difference out of your own pocket.

I just hate the way this old furniture is going to look in my new house.

Let's face it, we all have become used to the furniture in our homes. Whether you've had that sofa for 4 years or 40 years, it really hasn't bothered you until now. Now, when you think about having the moving company relocate that old plaid "beast" into your brand new house, it really makes you think. If you think that having that new living room setup is something you can't live without, think for a minute about how it might affect your mortgage loan approval. As we've already mentioned in several sections regarding increased expenses, your loan approval may or may not be affected by racking up additional debt. You likely will, however, cause yourself some delay in the process as this new information must now be documented and sent back to your mortgage team for review and approval.

Your best bet is to get into the house first, and then decide what looks best and what you can afford. This also will give you an opportunity to see how what you "thought" would look best will really look. You also will have a better idea of your monthly expenses and can make an informed purchase that will better fit your budget. You also may actually find that the perfect sectional you picked out is simply too large to fit in the living room.

But, I thought we were getting
along so well...

Regardless of how well you plan out your life, things happen. For example, you may find yourself in a situation where you have either been laid off or "right-sized" through a corporate restructuring. It's difficult enough to have this happen anyway, much more so if you are in the middle of qualifying for a mortgage for the purchase of a new home. But as with all things, there may be an opportunity in this otherwise difficult circumstance. Switching jobs in the middle of your mortgage process will not necessarily disqualify you for your new home loan, but as we've seen already, it likely will cause you a bit of a delay as you find, land and start your new position.

The important thing to remember if this should happen to you is to try and stay in the same line of work that you have been in to this point. For example, if you are a Brain Surgeon who has been dropped by the local hospital due to budgetary cutbacks (like that would ever happen!), it doesn't make sense for you to use this as an opportunity to "find yourself" in your new career as a Yoga Instructor! While this may be your passion and may come with much less stress, it likely will not provide you with the same level of income that you had previously enjoyed while on staff at the hospital. This is an extreme example, but one worth thinking through if you find yourself in this situation. Remember – making a move may not necessarily disqualify you for a mortgage, but it likely will delay the process. Be sure to check your Purchase Contract for details and deadlines, and keep your mortgage team and your Realtor informed as you look to get back on your feet.

Timmy just graduated, and we wanted to surprise him with a new car!

We are all proud of our kids. Heck, there are not many things that we wouldn't do to provide a better future for those we've been entrusted to raise. But when you are in the middle of qualifying for a new home loan, it's important to remember that somebody else is reviewing your financial condition, and you really need to be cautious when it comes to adding expenses to your budget. Yes, you may have a plan to "pay this off after the tax refund comes back next year", but you still are incurring a new monthly obligation to repay a debt today.

If you still feel that you must go through with the purchase of the new car for Timmy, it's ultimately your call, but you can be sure that your mortgage team will find out – they have ways of catching these things! Once that happens, they will need the paperwork to support the new monthly payment obligation. As we've already mentioned in the "I deserve a new car" discussion, this may or may not disqualify you for the new home loan you are seeking. It will, however, most likely cause a delay in the process. My advice to you is to just be patient. If Timmy is as smart as you think he is, he will understand if the car comes a month after graduation.

There's WHAT wrong with the house?!?

Sometimes it happens. You've found the "perfect" new home for your family and everyone has fallen in love with it. It's in the right school district, close to shopping and even has that third car garage that you've always dreamed of. Nothing could go wrong with this, right? Well maybe. Both sellers and Realtors are legally responsible to let potential buyers know if there are "known" issues with a home listed for sale. The potential here is for those "unknown unknowns" to pop up and catch everyone off-guard. Through the mortgage loan process, we've already discussed that the mortgage team will hire an independent third party (the Appraiser) to give an objective view of the current market value of the home. This protects the lender from loaning money on an inflated sales price that may or may not be representative of the current market environment.

This process also protects the potential

buyer of the house, by providing an objective (but professional) opinion of value which ensures that you don't pay more than the house is actually worth. For example, if you found a home next door to your brother and just HAD to have it, you may be willing to pay whatever the owner wants for the convenience of having your brother as your next-door neighbor. In this example, it would be worth the investment for you to be able to live so close to your brother, but the house may not be worth as much to someone like me, who doesn't know your brother from Adam.

Since the professional Appraiser is responsible for the measurement, review and (basic) visual inspection of the house, he or she may also come across issues with the property that were previously unknown by either the seller or the Realtor listing the home for sale. These could include termite infestation, faulty wiring or plumbing or rotted wood in the attic, which could create a safety hazard for the occupants of the house. These things in and of themselves may not necessarily cause your deal to fall apart, but they certainly will mean more conversations about who will be responsible to pay for fixing them and how long that may or may not delay the mortgage process.

How Are Interest Rates Determined?

So, you've made the first move by applying for a home mortgage with a licensed mortgage professional. Good for you! If and when the topic of interest rates came up, were you surprised, curious or indifferent?

If you are like most Americans, you don't really even think about interest rates unless you are trying to purchase a new car, get a new credit card or obtain something else on credit. This subject applies to home loans as well. And while your mortgage professional can be a great resource for understanding what the current mortgage interest rate environment is, precious few of them actually understand what goes into setting the interest rates on a daily basis.

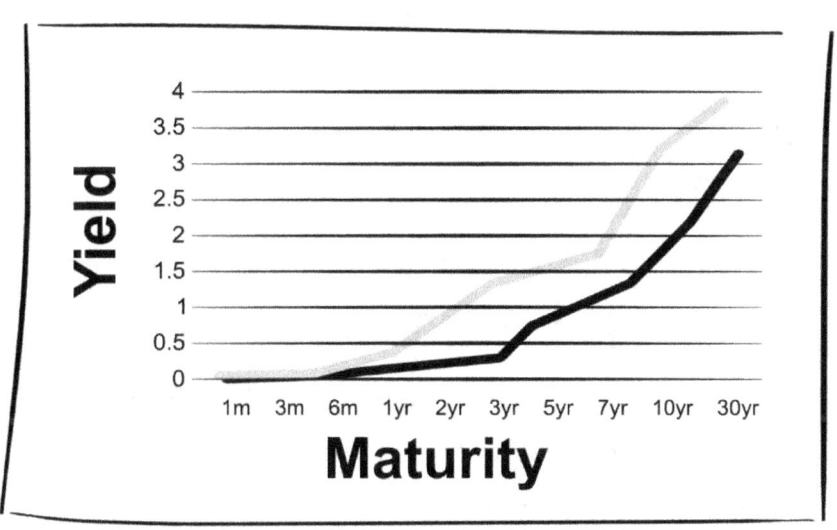

What are Short-term and Long-term Treasuries?

Before we get into the details of how mortgage interest rates are set each day, we need to set up a few definitions to lay the ground work for the rest of this chapter. Every day, the United States Government purchases and sells short-term Treasury bills (periods of a few days to 52 weeks) and longer-term Treasury bonds (maturities of 10 to 30 years). In either case, the longer the maturity, the higher the interest rate ("yield") that is due to Investors in these types of instruments. This readily-available trading of bills and bonds provides an environment where investing in (and getting rid of) these instruments is relatively easy and creates a "liquid" marketplace for Investors in these types of instruments.

In addition to these instruments which are issued by the United States Government, there also exists a "liquid" marketplace for mortgage-backed securities (MBS). These come in the form of either Agency-issued securities (Ginnie Mae, Fannie Mae or Freddie Mac) or non-Agency issued (Jumbo or other non-QM mortgage-backed) and are typically traded and available for purchase or sale on a daily basis. These are typically set up on a "pass-through" basis, meaning that the Principal and Interest payments made by the mortgage holder (borrower) are "passed through" to the owner of the MBS (the Investor – we will define this next), with a portion of the actual Interest charged being earned by the Servicer and a portion going to the Agency issuing the security.

For simplicity, we will assume that there is a .50% difference between the mortgage Interest Rate paid by the borrower and the pass-through rate earned by the MBS Investor, with .25% of that going to the Servicer of record and .25% going to the Agency issuing the MBS.

For example: Your mortgage Interest Rate is 4.50% and the pass-through rate is 4.00%. What this means is that each month when you pay your monthly mortgage payment, 4.00% goes to the MBS Investor, .25% goes to the Servicer and .25% goes to the Agency (Ginnie Mae, Fannie Mae or Freddie Mac).

Mortgage-backed Securities Investors Defined

Thirty years ago, unless you were a wealthy individual with at least $25,000 to invest, you would have a hard time investing in Agency-issued mortgage-backed securities. Today, that same $25,000 option still exists for Ginnie Mae MBS, but savvy Investors can partake in Conventional (Fannie Mae and Freddie Mac) MBS purchases for as little as $1,000. This can be a pretty good way to earn interest income based on the current depository interest rate environment. Would you rather earn .50% on a depository account at your local bank or 4.00% on your portion of a MBS?

There are some things to remember if you plan to invest in mortgage-backed securities, however. Even though you can invest in securities with terms of up to 30 years, you may not receive the same income stream for a full 30 years. For example, in a falling interest rate environment, borrowers will tend to refinance their existing loans in order to take advantage of lower interest rates. If the security you hold contains mortgages that prepay ("run off') before the end of their expected term, your resulting income will go down as a proportion of the total MBS pool. If this prepayment occurs, as an Investor in the MBS, you are guaranteed to get your Principal back, but you may not continue to receive the Interest income if the underlying mortgages have all prepaid.

In the same way, in a rising interest rate environment, borrowers are less likely to refinance their existing mortgages. The problem with this is that as an Investor in a mortgage-backed security you are locked in to a rate of return on your MBS as long as you hold that MBS. If the interest rates available in other investment alternatives become more attractive as rates increase, you will need to sell your current MBS holding. The challenge is that your sale will likely be at a discount since the rate of return would be less than another Investor can get in the current market environment. Even though there is a liquid market for Agency-issued MBS, the market is also competitive and stable, meaning that a reasonable Investor will not pay more for something than it is actually worth.

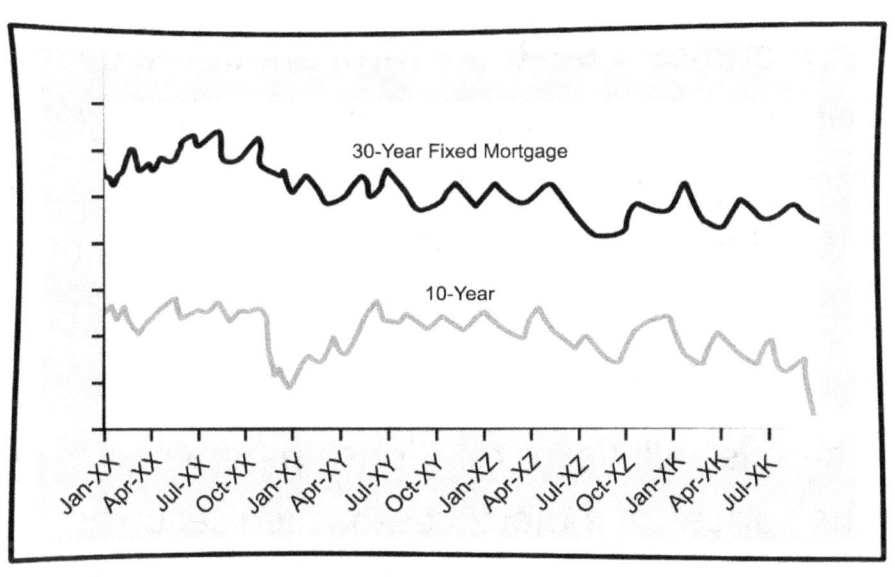

Mortgage Rates Compared to Mortgage-backed Securities Rates

We have already defined for simplicity sake that there is a .50% difference between mortgage rates (the interest rate that borrowers pay) and MBS yields (the interest rate that Investors receive). Knowing this, mortgage rates will fluctuate daily (sometimes repeatedly throughout the day) with the corresponding movement of mortgage-backed securities. Let's dive a little deeper into the movement of MBS and some of the things that can affect the rising or lowering of rates in the market today.

There is an inverse relationship between the "price" of a mortgage-backed security and the "yield" received by Investors in that same MBS. Better stated, the higher the price – the lower the yield and vice versa. If you've ever had an Economics course in school (and even if you have not), you may be familiar with the law of supply and demand. It basically says the more something is in demand, the higher the price someone is willing to pay for it. If prices continue to increase to a level where they just don't make financial sense, demand will slow and the prices will come back to a "reasonable" level. This is what makes for an efficient marketplace for anything from houses to cars to baseball cards. The more efficient the marketplace, the more quickly prices (and in our example – interest rates) will move to find an efficient level.

To use our MBS example, let's suppose you invest in a Fannie Mae MBS with a yield of 4.00% and that you pay par (100.00) for that particular "current coupon". This means that in an efficient marketplace, a 4.00% yield Fannie Mae MBS sells for exactly its Face Value (no premium paid or discount charged by the current seller of the MBS). If interest rates go up and the current coupon becomes 4.50%, your current holding of 4.00% will be less valuable because Investors can purchase a higher yielding security in the current market. Your 4.00% MBS will be devalued and will sell at a discount because a "reasonable" Investor will not pay more for something than it is truly worth. So, I might offer you 98% of the current Face Value for your MBS because I know I will only receive 4.00% in yield on it once I own it.

As you can see, this topic gets very confusing very quickly, and we could complete an entire book using just this example. For now, let's continue our discussion of mortgage interest rates so that we can provide some more clarity on where they come from and how they are set.

I've Seen Rates Quoted in the News. Why Can't I Get Those Rates?

Whether it's Bank Rate, Lending Tree or the local nightly news attempting to distill down to a headline the current interest rate environment, there is no shortage of data regarding current mortgage interest rates. The problem with many of these rate quotes (even some of those on-line) is that there simply is a delay from the time the information is gathered to the time it is published to the general population. For printed media, the delay from data gathering to printing deadline to actual production to delivery to the retail outlet can be anywhere from a week to a month. As we've already discussed, interest rates change daily – and in some instances, multiple times throughout the day. Knowing this, there is very little chance that the interest rates published in hard copy format are actually available.

Information distributed via television or radio tends to be more timely but still contains an inherent delay from data gathering to broadcast. Interest rates published on the Internet have a better chance of providing current data, but the source for this data usually is not readily known. For example, an on-line mortgage Lender may have a real-time feed updating their rates automatically throughout the day. This would be the best source for valid information at any given time. However, there are a multitude of Lenders who publish their interest rates on-line but who only update this information once each day (or each week). Carefully check the fine print when relying on Internet-based mortgage rates.

OK, so let's assume the rates you see on the news are accurate. Let's also assume that you see them the exact moment that they are published, and you have the most current information available to any borrower regarding interest rates. What about the fine print on those quotes? Many times, Lenders want to provide their absolute best quote when providing rates to the public. This will most likely come with specific qualifying details that must be outlined in the rate quote. Details such as minimum Credit Score, maximum Loan to Value (LTV), maximum Debt to Income (DTI) or minimum Loan Amount are a few that could make the published quote something lower than you are actually looking for.

For example, let's say a Lender publishes a rate of 4.50% today but displays the following in their "fine print":

> Minimum Credit Score of 780, maximum LTV of 80% and maximum DTI of 35%.

If you are a first-time homebuyer looking for a mortgage with the lowest down payment, you might meet the Credit Score and DTI barriers, but you haven't yet saved up 20% of the Purchase Price for down payment. Your rate will generally be higher. By contrast, you might have as much as 30% to put down on the purchase of your new home, but your Credit Score is only 680. This will also push you into a higher interest rate bracket.

I'm a Successful Real Estate Investor. Why Is My Rate Higher?

Yes, you know what you are doing! There, that's out of the way. Now, let's talk about mortgages in general. Generally speaking, someone who actually lives in the home they are putting up as collateral for a mortgage has a higher propensity to repay the debt, even if their finances are stretched. They do this because everyone needs someplace to live, right? So it does stand to reason that a non-owner occupied house would pose a greater risk of non-payment, everything else being equal. It is for this general reason that even experienced Real Estate Investors are saddled with higher down payment requirements and generally higher interest rates.

Don't be discouraged, though. As a successful Real Estate Investor, you also have access to lending options that a first-time homebuyer doesn't have. For example, there are products available today that allow for qualification based SOLELY on the Debt Coverage Ratio (DCR) of the subject property. This means that as long as the rent you are collecting on the subject property is enough to cover the monthly Principal, Interest, Taxes, Insurance and Association Dues – if any (PITIA), you don't even need to tell the Lender WHERE you work, HOW MUCH you make or even IF you work. There, don't you feel better now?

What REALLY Happened During the Crash?

It's entirely possible that you are reading this and truly have no idea that we had a "Crash" in the Real Estate market just over 10 years ago. For example, if you are 25 years old now and are looking to buy your first home with your spouse, you would have been 15 when this happened and more concerned about your date for this weekend than anything else. A "housing crisis" would have been the last thing on your mind.

Risky Features

The mortgage industry has learned much over these past 10 years. Some of what we learned was due to an extreme collapse of our way of earning a living, and some of it was forced on us in the form of Government oversight and increased financial regulation. To be fair, I'm all for regulation. Mankind has shown time and time again that, left to our own devices we will not look out for anyone but ourselves. Of course, this is an over-generalization, and there are (still) some very high-caliber people in the mortgage business. The ones I am referring to are those who took loans with already risky features and sold them to folks who had no business qualifying for them in the first place.

One of these risky features involved the delivery of interest-only loans, where the monthly mortgage payment only went toward the interest charged by the Lender. These loans provided a much lower monthly payment but provided NO equity accumulation on the underlying house. For example, if the housing market had remained unchanged from the time you obtained an interest-only loan, when it came time to sell your house or refinance that loan, the only equity you would have had in your home would have been the down payment that was required when your first purchased the property.

Another risky feature, and a likely more "toxic" contributor to the meltdown, was the Option ARM. This loan allowed the borrower to choose which option of monthly payment they wanted to make each month. One of these was enough to amortize the loan over 30 or 15 years, another was only enough to cover the interest on the loan (see interest-only above) and another actually was LOWER than that, allowing for a decrease in equity in the house. This last option is commonly known as Negative Amortization and virtually guaranteed an elimination of equity in a flat housing market. These loans had a built-in feature that demanded a review after 5 years, but at that point the damage had been done, and many homeowners found themselves in mortgages they could no longer afford with payments that had as much as doubled overnight.

Property Values Destroyed

Part of the reason for the crash was due to a quick decrease in property values across the country. Although this drop in values was widespread across the U.S., the decrease was led primarily by those properties located in so-called "sand states", like California, Nevada, Arizona and Florida. At issue was not necessarily that values just went down, but that they had gone up quite rapidly (sometimes as much as 20-30% per year!) in the 2-3 years leading up to this point. This created a need for some corrective movement in the valuation of Real Estate in order to get back to a level where reasonable Buyers and reasonable Sellers would be willing to exchange property. So, let's talk about what constitutes "reasonable" for a second.

When a willing Buyer and a willing Seller contract to transfer ownership of a property in a stable Real Estate market, the price of the property can be fairly estimated by looking at recent sales of similar properties near the subject property. These are called "comparable sales" by professional Real Estate Appraisers. In a market where property values are increasing rapidly, as we saw leading up to the crash, even the most professional Appraiser is estimating the value based on recent events and projections. Let me use an example of sports trading cards to explain. Let's assume that college football's number 1 draft pick has just signed with an NFL team. If you visit your local trading card shop, you might find that the price of this person's "rookie card" has just doubled because of the estimation of his impact on the league. Now let's think ahead 6 months to when the season is in full swing. Assume this same person has been arrested for several illegal activities, and his chance of playing again in the NFL has dropped to almost zero. The same rookie card you purchased a mere 6 months earlier would now be almost worthless, as the "star power" of that person has just vaporized.

Similarly, in an increasing Real Estate market, the promise of ever-increasing property values makes buying property easy, even if you do not intend to keep the property for the long-term. The fact that property values "have always gone up" (this was the mentality in the months/years leading up to the crash) means that you could not make a bad decision to purchase Real Estate. While my example of the pro football player is extreme, the housing market experienced a similar hit when property values quickly dropped.

Collateralized Debt Obligations and Other Exotic Financial Instruments

As we discussed already, there were a number of risky features that were designed and added to mortgage products in the early 2000s. I want to be clear that in my estimation, these features were not designed to punish borrowers. They were designed to provide ever-increasing yields for Investors who would purchase the rights to receive payments associated with the underlying mortgages.

In the search for increasing yields, several exotic financial instruments were created in an effort to make investing in mortgages both lucrative and available to a wide variety of Investors. One of these instruments is called a Collateralized Debt Obligation (CDO). According to Investopedia:

"A CDO is a type of financial instrument that pays investors out of a pool of revenue-generating sources. One way to imagine a CDO is a box into which monthly payments are made from multiple mortgages. It is usually divided into three tranches, each representing different risk levels.

As borrowers make payments on their mortgages, the box fills with cash. Once a threshold has been reached, such as 60% of the month's commitment, bottom-tranch investors are permitted to withdraw their shares. Commitment levels such as 80% or 90% may be the thresholds for higher-tranch investors to withdraw their shares. Bottom-tranch investing in CDOs is very attractive to institutional investors because the instrument pays better than T-Bills despite being considered almost risk-free."[1]

So, an investment in an asset (in this case, mortgage-backed securities) generally works well when the asset continues to increase in value.

[1] Investopedia ("Were Collateralized Debt Obligations (CDO) Responsible for the 2008 Financial Crisis" – October 20, 2017.

However, purchasing an asset that decreases in value – like that rookie card of the newly-convicted felon – generally does not produce a financial reward for anyone involved!

In addition to these types of instruments, Wall Street created other types of "exotic" financial instruments in an effort to continue to capitalize on the up-tick in values of mortgage-backed securities. Some of these included prepayment penalties, which are financial penalties due from the Borrower when loans are paid off before a certain period of time has passed. For example, in 2005 it was not uncommon to find loans that carried a 3-year prepayment penalty. This meant that if the loan was fully prepaid (or at least a substantial amount – generally more than 20% of the Unpaid Principal Balance) before the end of 3 years, the Borrower had to pay a penalty that was sometimes as much as 6 months' interest on the remaining Unpaid Principal Balance. This penalty assured MBS Investors that their income stream would continue for a minimum of 3 years, and if the underlying loans were prepaid within that period, they would receive a lump sum payment to offset the lack of earnings for the remaining 3 years.

The problem with these prepayment penalties was, in many cases, the Borrower had taken out an ARM loan that would adjust before the penalty period had elapsed. For example, suppose you took out a 2/28 LIBOR ARM loan in December of 2005 that contained a 3-year prepayment penalty. Your loan would have adjusted UPWARD in December 2007 (after the market had begun to decline) as much as 5% from the initial Note Rate. Since your loan contained a 3-year prepayment penalty, there would have been no way to refinance your loan without paying a substantial penalty for early payoff. In addition, during that time in the Real Estate market, your property value would likely have plummeted, so your ability to refinance into a more stable rate loan program would have been nonexistent. This was a big factor for many Borrowers "walking away" from their homes and mortgages during the early days of the Crash.

The Independent Mortgage
Banker's Role

In the early days of the Secondary Market, banks and savings and loans ruled the world. There had been decades of service to homebuyers for their financing needs by these institutions. The common philosophy was "If you need a home loan, go to your bank". This changed with the introduction of independent mortgage banks. These institutions worked with private mortgage insurance companies and others to create a vibrant and sustainable secondary market for mortgages. To clarify: The primary mortgage market is the relationship between the Borrower and the Lender; The secondary mortgage market is the relationship between the Lender and Investors in mortgage-backed securities.

As the independent mortgage banks continued to grow their market share, they proved to the borrowing world that they could provide an alternative to institutional financing for the purchase or refinance of mortgage loans. While these types of Lenders were certainly capable of providing mortgage financing, the regulation of them at a national level did not nearly compare with regulation facing banks and other institutional Lenders. This became evident during the Crash as independent mortgage bankers worked with Wall Street Investors to create a multitude of mortgage products that could literally meet any need a Borrower may have. These "creative" products helped to create a continuous flow of investment options for Wall Street, while providing some of the most flexible (and sometimes dangerous) alternatives for Borrowers.

As we have discussed a couple of times already, if the value of the underlying asset (in this case, Real Estate) continued to increase, there was no problem. When the market began to correct and folks began to "strategically default" on their mortgages,

Investors ran for cover and were no longer willing to purchase securities backed by mortgages closed under these creative conditions. When there no longer is a market filled with Buyers, Sellers can be left holding whatever inventory they have accumulated. Do you remember "fidget spinners"? It seemed like virtually overnight they were the latest craze, and if you were looking for one for your kids, there were none to be purchased at any price. Fast forward to a year later and they can be purchased for pennies because demand for them has not kept up with the supply. If an entrepreneurial person saw the wave a year ago and ordered a million of these to sell at a profit, that person could likely have several boxes left in their basement today!

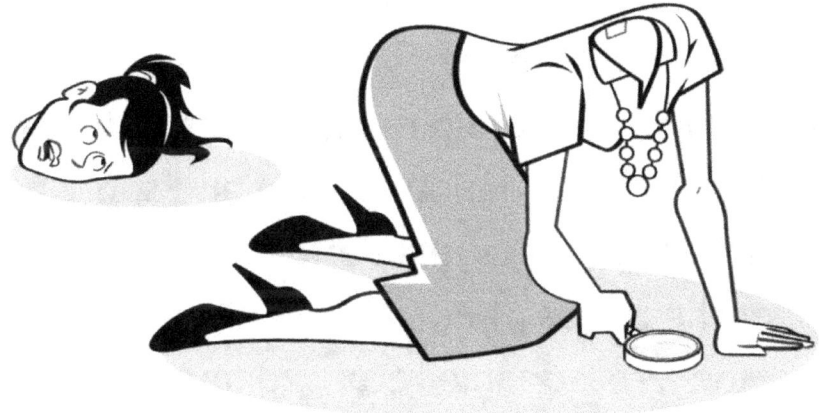

Did Everyone Lose Their Minds?!?

I had the opportunity to work in Product Development for a time leading up to the Crash. My job was to seek out multiple sources who were willing to purchase specific mortgage types and to create programs that could be offered to the general public that would match these requests. Since I am relatively risk-averse, I made sure that we had at least 2 to 3 sources who were willing to buy before creating and launching any new loan programs. I worked directly with Wall Street sources in the creation, pricing and sourcing of these loan types in an effort to not only meet the needs of Borrowers, but also provide a reasonable return to Investors who were willing to purchase securities backed by these mortgages. In the months leading up to the Crash, there was no shortage of Investors willing to entertain any number of "risky" features as long as

Lenders could provide an adequate supply of mortgages to support them.

When Real Estate prices began to drop, and when Borrowers began to strategically default on their mortgages, that supply of mortgages dried up quickly. In addition, the increasing number of defaults on these types of mortgages led to a de-valuing of the mortgage-backed securities that they were included with. This de-valuing led to a lower return for Investors and an unwillingness to continue to invest in securities backed by these mortgages. Much like the relative demise of the fidget spinner, securities backed by mortgages with "creative" features became something no one wanted to invest in. Virtually overnight the market for these mortgages dried up, and there were hundreds of Wall Street players and independent mortgage banks who closed their doors in a matter of a few months.

Today, it is relatively easy to look back and ask if everyone lost their minds. I would argue that the secondary mortgage market was simply attempting to meet the needs of the borrowing public. In retrospect, there were a number of risky things taking place with virtually no government oversight in mortgage lending. Now I'm not normally one for government oversight, but in this case, it could have made the difference between the success or failure of the Real Estate lending market.

What the Government Did to Make
Sure It Doesn't Happen Again

As I mentioned previously, there was a dramatic difference between the oversight of depository institutions and that of independent mortgage bankers. Please understand that I don't see the independent mortgage bank as some type of "aggressive manipulator", with no regard for risk or long-term consequences. I have spent my professional life working for independent mortgage banks and I fully agree with the philosophy behind why they were created and why they continue to thrive. I do recognize, however, that without some level of government oversight it becomes possible for a few "bad actors" to manipulate the system and find ways to earn a living without regard to potential consequences.

In July 2010, following passage of the Dodd-Frank Wall Street Reform and Consumer Protection Act, the Consumer Financial Protection Bureau (CFPB) was created. The responsibility of the CFPB was to consolidate oversight of a number of other federal regulatory bodies, including the Federal Reserve, the Federal Trade Commission, the Federal Deposit Insurance Corporation, the National Credit Union Administration and the Department of Housing and Urban Development. Their primary goal is to "watch out for American consumers in the market for consumer financial products and services."[2]

While we have learned much from the past 10 years, I believe that mortgage lending still needs to be diligent in efforts to ensure a vibrant secondary market while limiting the potential risk to the borrowing public. This was attempted in the past as a type of self-policing, but there simply needed to be more accountability.

---

[2] Consumer Financial Protection Bureau website –
https://www.consumerfinance.gov/about-us/the-bureau/creatingthebureau/

Simply stated, independent mortgage bankers now have accountability that is more in line with others who lend money to the American consumer. I think that is a good thing for everyone.

What Types of Loans are Available?

OK, you are ready to get started! But what is the best loan type for you? There really is something for everyone. Regardless of your financial and housing goals, chances are there is a product that is absolutely perfect for what you want to accomplish. Having said that, I want to be clear that not every loan product is perfect for every borrower. We will discuss in another chapter in greater detail what happens when the wrong person attempts to purchase a home using the wrong loan program. For now, let's take a look at several options available in the current marketplace and find out what option(s) might be right for you.

Purchase money loans

If you have found the home of your dreams that you would like to move your family in to, regardless of whether or not you currently own a home, you are talking about financing for the purchase of your new home (unless you are planning to pay cash for the whole thing). The process typically works like this: You either find a home for sale in an area that you would like to live by searching the Internet or by using the services of a licensed Realtor. You make an offer to purchase the home through your Realtor who then draws up the necessary offer paperwork and presents it to the Listing Agent (or to the seller directly, in the case of a For Sale by Owner, or "FSBO" transaction). Once your offer has been accepted, you now have a specified timeframe during which you must either pay cash or obtain financing for the home. If you've worked with a mortgage professional in the past, you probably already know someone who can help. If you do not, your Realtor can certainly recommend a qualified professional who will help you through the process.

I would like to interject a personal opinion here, since it's my book, and I can. The value of a Realtor cannot be overstated for the buyer in a purchase transaction. You may think that the seller of the home you love would take a lower offer price for the house if you didn't use your own Realtor, but the seller will pay a commission regardless of who helps you purchase the home. If you don't have your own representation, the seller's Realtor will earn the whole commission and will do their best to be impartial since they would be representing both you AND the seller in the transaction. This is called dual agency and is completely legal, but it can be tricky when it comes to matters of confidence. Just be careful and don't overlook the value of having your own representation in likely the largest financial move you will make in your lifetime.

Refinancing – Both for cash-out and to lower payments

If you currently own your home (or at least are making payments to someone to purchase it over time), you may have an opportunity to refinance your existing mortgage if it makes financial sense for you to do so. Reasons for this could be that you have a child graduating high school who is off to Harvard, and you can't imagine saddling your baby with a mountain of student loan debt to pay off once they graduate. Or, you might have just turned 50 and saw the hottest red corvette you've ever seen, and you just have to have it. By the way, I wouldn't recommend taking cash out of your primary residence to purchase a depreciating asset like a car, no matter how hot it looks! On the more practical side, perhaps your house could use some updating like a new kitchen or bathroom. These things really add value to your home, but they don't come cheap.

There also may be a valid reason to refinance your existing mortgage when you have no interest in borrowing even more money. Perhaps the interest rates have dropped to a level below where your current mortgage rate is, and you have the ability to simply lower your rate, payments or term by refinancing. If you are thinking about refinancing, just make sure that it makes financial sense for you to do it. If you refinance your existing loan, there will generally be costs associated with the refinance. You can either pay these out of pocket, take a higher interest rate so that the Lender can give you a credit to pay them or you can finance them into the new loan amount. Any way you look at it, there will be a cost associated with a new loan. Just be sure that your monthly savings will be enough to cover these costs during the time you expect to be in the home.

Fixed rate loans

These are the "bread and butter" of mortgage lending. Fixed rate loans have been around since the 1970s and provide a constant, fixed interest rate over the life of the mortgage loan. Generally speaking, first-time homebuyers and people with a low tolerance for risk are great candidates for fixed rate loans. They provide security for the long-term and consistency in the way equity is built in the underlying property. A fixed rate loan might also be good for an Investor seeking to acquire a property to rent out who wants a certain monthly payment so that cash flows can be reasonably estimated.

Although a fixed rate loan has a consistent Principal and Interest payment over the life of the loan, there may be instances where the monthly payment could go up (or down). Things such as an increase in property taxes can cause the monthly mortgage payment to go up. Generally speaking, each municipality reviews property taxes annually to determine if the current tax rate is sufficient for the current market environment. When this happens in an improving Real Estate market, taxes will usually go up. If your taxes and insurance are paid each month as a part of your regular escrow account payment, when your mortgage servicer evaluates your escrow account at the end of the year, your monthly portion for taxes and insurance will have to go up so that you have a sufficient balance in your escrow account to make the tax payment. This same logic will hold for any type of increase in property insurance or the addition of a requirement to carry flood insurance on your property that may not have existed when you first took out the mortgage.

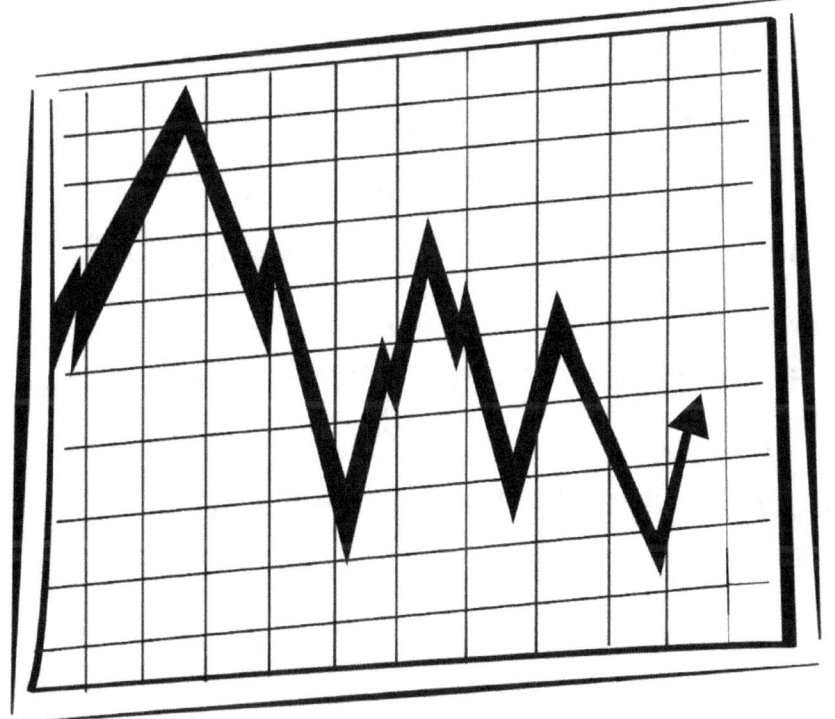

Adjustable rate loans

If fixed rate loans are the bread and butter of mortgage lending, then adjustable rate mortgages (also known as "ARMs") could be seen as the peas and carrots. While not necessarily made for every person, ARMs can be very useful for the right circumstances. ARMs typically have a fixed interest rate for an introductory period and then adjust based on market conditions at pre-determined intervals. For example, a 1-year ARM is fixed for one year and then adjusts every year after the initial twelve months. A 3/1 ARM is fixed for the first three years and then adjusts every year after the initial 36 months.

If you think an ARM might be right for you, just consider the risks associated with them. In a rising interest rate environment, when your ARM rate adjusts it will likely go up, resulting in higher mortgage payments each month. Additionally, as we mentioned in the fixed rate loans section, your property could also be subject to higher taxes or insurance payments which could magnify any increase in monthly payment due to an increase in your interest rate. I know all of this sounds like I'm against ARMs, but there are some really good reasons to choose an ARM.

Interest rates on ARMs are generally lower than they are for fixed rate loans. The reason for this is the risk involved with a potential increase in your interest rate during the life of your loan. If you believe that interest rates are going to remain stable or go down, then an ARM would be a wise choice because as the rates go down, so will your monthly mortgage payment. Also, there are a number of "hybrid" ARMs available today that could fit with your Real Estate investment strategy. For example, a 3/1 or 5/1 ARM could be right for you if your plan is to stay in the home (or at least in the mortgage) for three or five years. If you are a Real Estate investor purchasing a rental property that you intend to sell after four years, a 5/1 ARM could be just what you need. Your interest rate will be fixed for the first five years and your plan is to liquidate your holding in that property before the interest rate adjusts.

Non-QM loans

In January, 2013, the Consumer Financial Protection Bureau (CFPB) first issued the definition of a Qualified Mortgage ("QM"). This definition not only assumed that the Lender followed the ability-to-repay ("ATR") rule, but also included the following:

- No risky loan features
    - No interest-only loans
    - No negative amortization loans
    - No balloon payments
    - No loan terms longer than 30 years
- A limit on how much of your income can go toward your debt (DTI ratio)
- No excess upfront points and fees
    - Generally speaking, the maximum fees that can be charged to a borrower is 3% of the loan amount
- Certain loans originated during a transitional period if they are eligible for purchase or guarantee by Fannie

Mae or Freddie Mac (the government-sponsored enterprises "GSEs"). The transitional period is set to expire on the earlier of the date that the GSEs exit federal conservatorship or receivership or on January 10, 2021. OK, so what does all of this mean? The federal government has outlined a series of definitions in an effort to protect consumers from issues that contributed to the mortgage meltdown of 2007-2008 – which we discuss in detail in another chapter. The above referenced definition is meant to protect consumers from bad behavior that might ultimately harm them financially.

While the creation of this rule made sense, it did have the unintended consequence of restricting credit to otherwise credit-worthy borrowers. Early 2013 saw many Lenders pull back from all but the most conservative approaches to underwriting. Otherwise credit-worthy borrowers were being hindered from purchasing a new home because of the limitations being imposed on creditors across the country. Lately, we have begun to see the re-emergence of some of these types of loans.

Non-QM loans, as they are known to the mortgage industry, are those loans that do not fit with the CFPB definition as presented here. This is not to say that these are bad loans, or even closely associated with the types of bad behavior that led to the mortgage meltdown. There are many reasons that a borrower may not qualify for a QM loan today. Part of the CFPB guidance on the issue requires that Lenders document a borrower's ability to repay their mortgage debt. If a borrower has an inconsistent income source, or perhaps uses the current tax laws to minimize their income tax liability, they could find themselves in a situation where documentation of a stable, continuous source of income cannot be documented. In these cases, without a non-QM option, they would not be able to borrow money to purchase or refinance their home.

Another non-QM source for mortgage help is private-money financing – also known as "hard money" lending. These types of loans can be a good option for those whose plan for holding the underlying Real Estate is for the short term. Generally, hard money loans carry with them much higher interest rates and fees than do traditional secondary market-eligible loans. They also tend to have a much shorter time horizon, since private investors usually want to recoup their investment in a shorter timeframe. Having said that, these types of loans can generally close much faster than a traditional mortgage and will carry a much lower burden of documentation.

Construction-type loans

If purchasing a brand-new home is in your budget, you may have the option of borrowing using a construction-to-permanent mortgage. These loans will provide financing for the purchase or payoff of the lot where the home will be built while also providing funding to the Builder for the construction of the completed residence. The benefit of this type of lending is that the borrower is placed on title to the property upfront, and there is no risk that the Builder will change his/her mind once construction has begun and decide to sell the home to someone else. The risk is that interest rates are generally not guaranteed upfront, so the final interest rate on the loan will be subject to the prevailing rates at the time construction is completed on the residence. Also, for Conventional financing, borrowers generally need to be prepared to have at least 20% equity in the property. This could come from a current appraisal report or from a significant cash down payment to the Lender.

By contrast, you might have found a home in the perfect location, but it is need of some serious rehabilitation work. In this case, you might be a candidate for a renovation loan, such as an FHA 203(k). These mortgages will provide for minor (or sometimes major) repairs to the subject property and can be obtained with a lower down payment than is required for Conventional financing. Another advantage of the FHA 203(k) is that the interest rate can be guaranteed upfront, so there is no risk of interest rates increasing before the renovation work is completed. Details for this particular program are extensive, so we will not cover more than this high-level discussion here.

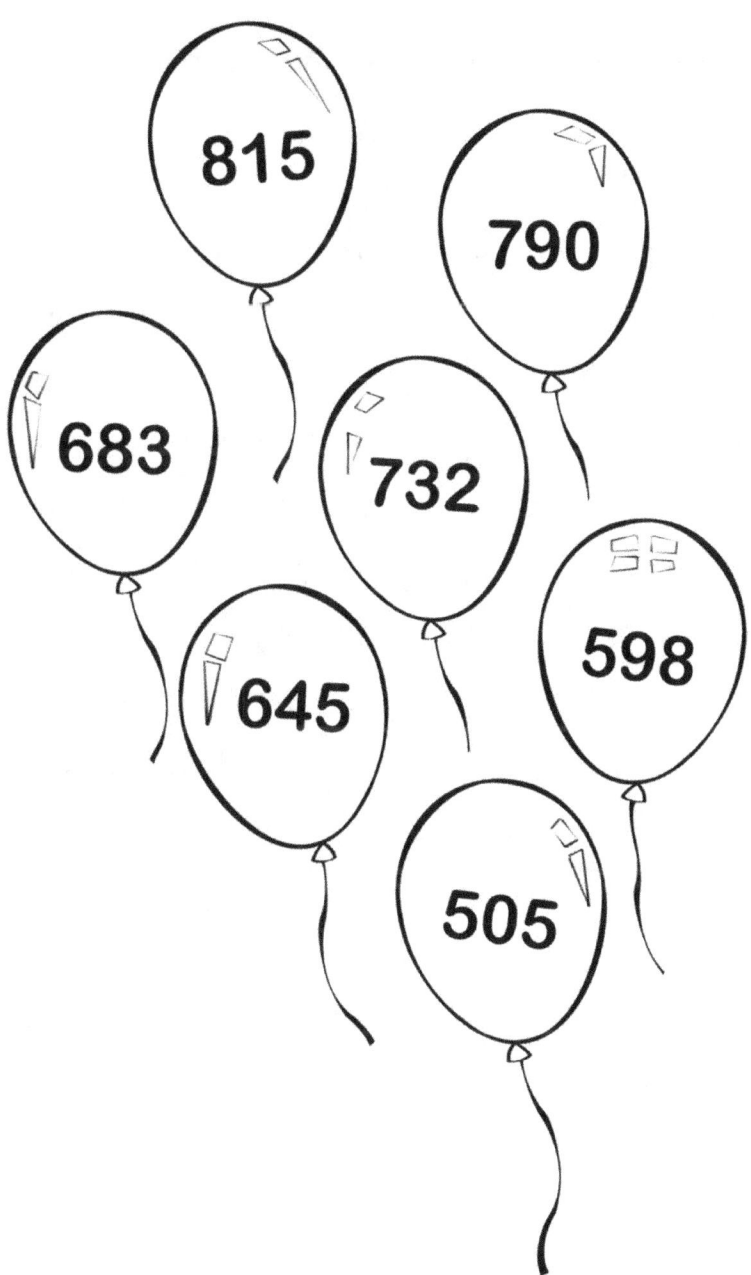

What's In A Credit Score?

Your credit score. That mysterious little demon that can make you dance in the street or sulk in the shadows. Even the folks at Credit Karma[3] are getting into the game with their newest advertising campaign by playing on our fears of the unknown about our credit score. Regardless of how you feel about your credit score, it has become a very important part of lending over the past 20 years. The short answer is this: If you have a high credit score, the odds are good that you will repay your debts and you will be offered more debt than you ever care to carry. By contrast, if you have a low credit score, you are generally less likely (according to the scoring models) to pay your bills on time and thus, less likely to be offered credit on favorable terms.

---

[3] Credit Karma is a registered trademark of Credit Karma, Inc. Neither the Author nor JW Mortgage Group, LLC have any relationship with or interest in Credit Karma.

What really goes into making up my credit score?

Let's start with a couple of definitions. There are three different credit repositories (or bureaus) in the United States: Experian, Equifax and TransUnion – That's it! Creditors across the country who choose to report payment history on loans they service to these repositories can choose to either report to only one (which is cheaper and requires less paperwork) or to all three. There are actually geographic pockets in the country where many of the creditors who only report to one bureau all seem to report to the same one. In the case of mortgages, since there is a chance that your payment to Bob's Furniture Store in Mobile, Alabama may only be reported to one of the three bureaus, Lenders will always default to pulling all three bureaus' information (and score) so that they can be sure to capture your COMPLETE payment history. To be clear, when mortgage Lenders use the term "credit score" they are talking about the middle of three scores or the lower of two scores, if you only have two scores.

Having said all of this, each bureau has their own formula for determining the credit worthiness of each of us. The real thing to remember is that there are different calculations depending on what type of lending institution is looking at your credit – whether that is a credit card provider, a new car dealership or a mortgage broker. For example, a bank financing your new car purchase is really interested in your overall payment history, but their risk is limited to the potential repossession of your car if you should fail to make your payments. Cars are personal property, and while some of us treat them better than we treat our own children (you know who you are!), financial institutions have a much easier time taking your car back than they do your house. When it comes to Real Estate, however, the laws are much more strict and Lenders must use a much higher level of review when determining whether or not to loan you money.

In addition, your credit scores will likely change every time a new credit check is performed on you. While the bureaus have accounted for things like car shopping, getting pre-approved for a mortgage and other "normal" behavior, there can be a difference in scores for you every time someone else pulls your credit.

I've checked Credit Karma and I know what my score is.

Let me start by saying that I have no feelings, either positive or negative, about Credit Karma. I understand that they have developed a huge following since their inception in 2006, and they appear to be successfully leveraging advertising media to generate an even greater use of their product. According to their website, Credit Karma provides access to your credit scores from TransUnion and Equifax. They then will make recommendations to you as a member to borrow from one of the banks or lenders in the Credit Karma network. If you choose to do business with their partners, then Credit Karma earns a fee for referring you to them. That's why the service is free for you to use. They get paid by their referral partners.

Now, I can tell you what Credit Karma is NOT. They are not a bank, Lender or any other type of credit provider. They simply gather data from two of the three credit bureaus (Why not all three? I'm not sure.) and then market bank and Lender products to you as a member. And when it comes to Real Estate Finance, we've already discussed that the formula for determining the credit score of an individual for the purposes of mortgage lending are more restrictive than they are for consumer debt. So, even if you know exactly what your Credit Karma scores are, there is nearly a 100% chance that they will be different when your mortgage Team accesses the information.

This does not mean that Credit Karma is bad. I firmly believe in the value of being an informed consumer. Heck, that's why I'm writing this book! If you choose to use Credit Karma to monitor your credit activity, and if you can put up with the recommendations from their referral partners, then I think it always makes sense to be informed and aware of your credit surroundings. Just don't think that the numbers on Credit Karma are in any way tied to the numbers that your mortgage Team will share with you when it comes time for you to purchase your dream home or to refinance your existing mortgage. It's like comparing apples and watermelons.

Why doesn't the mortgage company just take my word for it?

You're a good person. You go to church on a pretty regular basis. You take care of your family, and you (mostly) pay your bills on time. What's not to trust? Please understand that the mortgage process is really NOT about trust. There's an old saying in lending: "It's not what you say, it's what you can document". This is not a trust issue between you and the Lender. I think that may be where the challenge is for many folks. They simply do not like the feeling that someone doesn't trust them. The reality is that the Lender is held to a standard of documentation that requires them to obtain documented proof of the claims they are making on your behalf when approving your loan. Your Lender must document your loan file so that in five or ten years, when some auditor in a basement of some government agency wants to dig into your file and make sure that the Lender did everything right, the documentation is right there to prove it.

I recently spent some time with Representatives from the Florida House of Representatives in Tallahassee. There were a number of issues on the agenda, but there seemed to be a common theme of putting laws in place because of a few bad actors. We've seen this at major sporting events also. If you haven't been to a game lately, the next time you go you should prepare for the same kind of screening you face when traveling by airplane. These precautions have been put into place because a few bad actors chose to behave improperly, so the rest of us are made to suffer. I don't think it's any different in lending. Because of the bad behavior of a few, those of us (you and me) who are just honest, hard-working people are forced to document our every move just to obtain financing for a place to call home. It's not right, but it's the world we live in.

How can I improve my credit score?

As we have already discussed, each of the three credit bureaus uses their own algorithm when calculating your score. In addition, that score could be different depending on the type of institution checking your credit – be it a credit card company, a bank or a mortgage Lender. There are some basics, however, that can help when it comes to raising your score – Regardless of the bureau or method used in coming up with your score. While simple things like paying off any collections accounts you may have will work, there generally is a time lag between when you pay those off and when they impact your credit score. When you meet with your mortgage Team and tell them "Oh, I've paid that off." (meaning that you mailed a check that morning to the credit company), chances are that it will take 30-45 days for that payment to be processed and the resulting effect to happen on your credit report.

Outstanding amount owed as a percentage of the total available credit is likely the area where you can get the biggest movement in the shortest amount of time. Generally speaking, the bureaus all look at each of your current active tradelines (individual accounts with the folks you've borrowed money from, and who you still owe money to), and compares the amount you owe to the total amount of credit you could possibly owe. For installment loans, like car notes and payments over a fixed period like the purchase of a new air conditioning unit, the balance goes down over time and usually never goes above what it currently shows on your credit report. Paying these off early may sound like a good idea, but they actually improve your score if you keep the amount owed at around 30% of the credit limit.

By contrast, with revolving loans (like credit card and "no interest for 90 days" accounts), there usually exists the possibility that you could increase the amount you owe if you either use your credit card or charge additional furniture to that 90-day account. In either of these cases, the creditor will set a maximum limit that you won't exceed, but as you pay down the amount due, you free up the ability to borrow more. Since these accounts are generally more expensive than installment loans, conventional wisdom says you should do all you can to pay them off first. Yes, this is always the best idea when dealing with high interest rate credit cards, but the same 30% rule will be in effect.

To sum up, if you have a credit card with a $10,000 credit limit and you owe $3,000 currently, your score will generally be better than if you owe $9,000 or $0 on that same account. Now I am not advocating that you carry debt you cannot afford. This section is merely to let you know some ways that you can improve your credit score.

Does it really matter what my credit score is?

The short answer is "Yes" – provided that obtaining credit on favorable terms is what you are after. The fact that you are still reading this book is probably a good indicator that you are someone who wants to get the best deal possible, and you are willing to do the research to make yourself an informed Consumer. If by contrast, you choose to pay cash for everything and really have no intention of borrowing from anyone – ever – then you might think that your credit score is irrelevant. If this is where you are in your financial life, let's talk about you for a second.

Credit, defined as our ability to have and to repay debt, affects nearly every area of our lives. Even folks who have vowed to NEVER use credit will feel the impact of their credit score whether they realize it or not. For example, it is generally a legal requirement that licensed motorists carry some type of liability insurance when they take to the road even if they choose not to carry comprehensive or collision insurance. Comprehensive and collision insurance covers your cost to repair your vehicle in case of an accident or other event and liability covers others' needs. The insurance industry uses your credit history as a gauge to determine the type of risk you present to them. If you are considered a high risk by the insuring agency (even if you don't consider yourself a high risk), you will generally pay a higher premium than someone they deem to be a lower risk than you.

Additionally, your choice to read this book indicates that you likely are at least curious about the Real Estate financing process. You (or a loved one) may not have the ability to pay cash for a new home, and it will become necessary to speak with a mortgage professional about applying for a home loan. I applaud you for taking the first step in educating yourself about this process and encourage you to seek wise counsel before you commit to borrowing at any level.

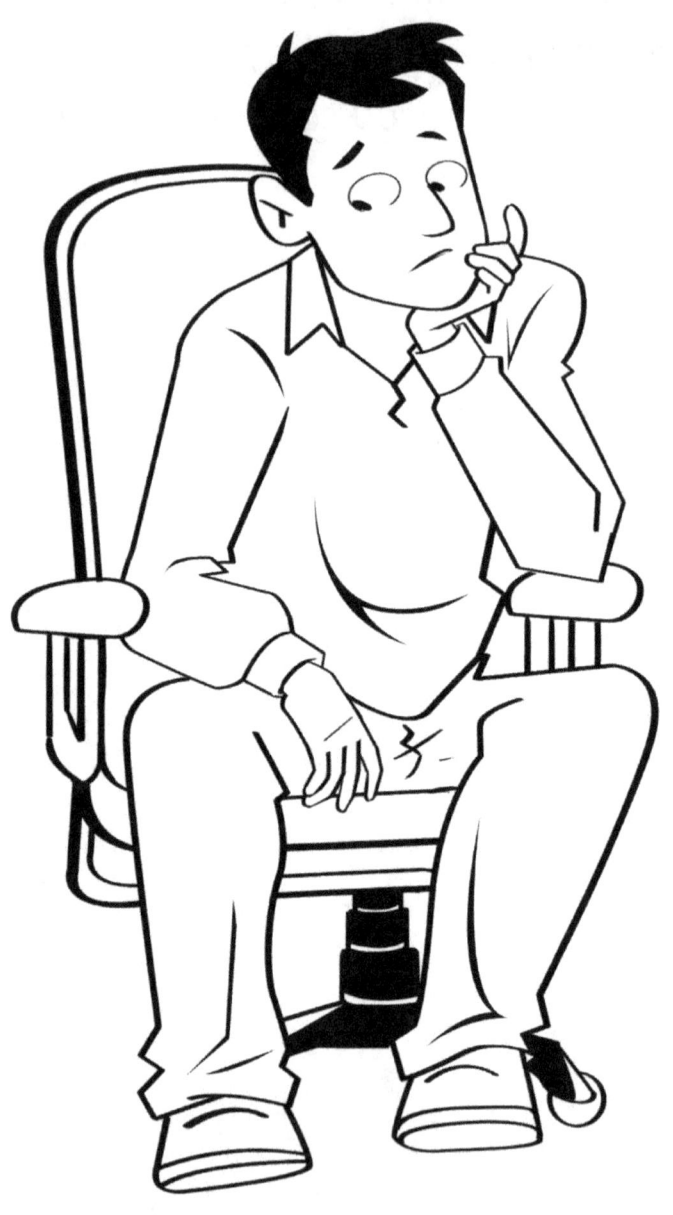

Are there any options for people with no credit score?

You may think that a credit score is like a fingerprint. Everyone has one. The reality is that credit scores are like personalities in that they develop over time. A person who has just graduated high school and has never used credit is a great example of someone who may genuinely NOT have a credit score. This does not make them a bad credit risk. It just means that they don't have a track record yet of being able to responsibly borrow and pay back money to others. Another reason for not having a credit score could be as a result of only borrowing from those creditors who choose not to report to one (or all) of the three credit bureaus. This might be a small "Buy Here, Pay Here" car dealership or a gym membership that generally won't report anything unless you fail to pay your bill.

Additionally, there may be individuals who are United States citizens but who have spent a majority of their lives living abroad.

Access to foreign credit does exist, but there is generally not a requirement for foreign creditors to report to the U.S. bureaus the activity of our citizens. This also holds true for people who are citizens of foreign countries. They may have a great track record of repayment in their home country, but they have never borrowed in the United States.

There are financing options for individuals who do not currently have a credit score. For the U.S. citizen, mortgage loans insured by the Federal Housing Administration (FHA) or loans from credit unions or other smaller lenders can be an option. For these folks, a "non-traditional" credit history can be developed by providing documentation of on-time payments for things like car insurance, cell phone and utility bills. Your mortgage Team can help you get this documentation to the right place so that your credit history can be developed.

For the foreign borrower wishing to purchase Real Estate in the United States, there are options which do not require a credit score. Keep in mind that these programs are generally considered "non-QM", which means that they do not have the same restrictions that a "Qualified Mortgage" carries in today's lending environment. They can be a great alternative, however, for getting started on the path to creating a credit history based in the United States.

Aren't All Mortgage Offices Basically the Same?

What's the difference in who you use for a mortgage? Doesn't everyone have access to the same information and the same loan programs? These are valid questions, and in this section we will take a look at some of the options available to you along with the pros and cons of each. I will take an objective look at each and promise to try not to steer you in a particular direction.

Banks

Since the first caveman chiseled out his initials on the first rock to signify his commitment to repay his cave loan, banks have ruled the lending world. OK, maybe that's a bit of a stretch. But I will say that banks have been lending since the beginning of banking. The simple math of it is that banks take in money in the form of deposits, which are currently insured by the Federal Deposit Insurance Corporation, or the National Credit Union Association, in the case of credit unions. Then they make loans to people to buy things they cannot afford to pay cash for. This could be for a new car, boat, motorcycle, or – for the topic of this book – a home. Generally speaking, most banks are allowed to borrow from the Federal Home Loan Bank at a discounted rate. They can then use that money to lend to folks like you and me at a slightly higher rate. The difference between their borrowing rate and the rate you and I pay is called "spread". In this over-simplified analogy, let's assume that a bank borrows at a rate of 1.50% (the current Fed Funds Rate) and then lends that same money to you at a rate of 4.50%. This creates a spread of 3.00%, which the bank uses to cover its monthly operating costs. On a loan amount of $100,000, this spread equates to roughly $3,000 per year – or $250 per month.

"But I've seen my bank building, and I know there is no way they can afford that with my measly $250 per month." you might say. Well, let's assume that there are others in your neighborhood who also need to borrow from the bank. Maybe there are 100 others, or maybe even 1,000. In that case, the bank is making roughly $250,000 per month in spread income, or $3 Million per year. Now that can definitely help pay for a fancy building. So, if that same bank has 15 branches that serve the same number of people at each branch, the dollar amounts add up quickly.

The positive side of going to your local bank for a mortgage loan is that they probably know you, your kids and your depository habits. This can be good for you, especially in the case where you might need them to make an exception to loan you money based on your credit score or debt to income ratio. If you have a significant history with them, they may be more apt to be flexible with your borrowing needs.

A potential drawback to using your local bank is that their employees are generally measured based on the number of products they can "cross sell" you on. If you are like me, you want to get in and get out and don't want to be "sold" on products you did not come in for. Another negative to using your bank for your mortgage needs is that mortgage lending is only a small part of what banks do every day. They also make car and boat loans, issue credit and debit cards and may also provide investment counseling and services. If their total focus is not on mortgages, they could miss important details that might stand out to those who focus solely on mortgage lending.

Non-bank Mortgage Lenders

As an alternative to going to the bank for a mortgage loan, you have the option to deal with a non-bank mortgage Lender. These companies are not depository institutions, so they do not make their money by taking in deposits, nor do they have the ability to borrow from the Federal Home Loan Bank system. These Lenders typically borrow from a warehouse bank, which is an institution that will make a short-term commercial loan to provide funding while the underlying mortgage loan is closed and sold to an Investor in the secondary market. These Investors could include other non-bank mortgage Lenders, which are often called Aggregators, because they aggregate large pools of mortgages to hold in their servicing portfolio. Investors could also be Fannie Mae, Freddie Mac or Ginnie Mae, which are government-sponsored enterprises who account for a majority of the purchase of mortgage loans in the secondary market.

Non-bank mortgage Lenders generally set their daily mortgage interest rates based on current secondary market conditions. Therefore, rates set daily by non-bank Lenders tend to more closely match actual market movements. This can be a benefit for potential Borrowers in an environment of rapidly improving (dropping) interest rates, where the Lenders typically will price to market each day. This would permit you, as the Borrower, to take advantage of lower rates. This same feature could also be a detriment in the case of a rising interest rate environment, where rates go up just as quickly as the market moves up.

An additional benefit to going through a non-bank mortgage Lender is the commitment they have made to doing ONLY mortgage loans. Where you typically would find credit cards, car loans, certificates of deposit and depository accounts at the corner bank, the non-bank mortgage lender gets to focus on doing only one thing. The concept here is that if they are focused on only one thing, they tend to get very good at that one thing. You also are not generally "up-sold" on other products when dealing with your licensed Mortgage Loan Originator in these environments.

A potential negative in using a non-bank mortgage Lender could be that you really do not have a relationship with the Lender. In that case, if something does not quite fit the lending mold for you, it could be difficult to obtain any type of exception to guidelines. Whereas your local bank may be able to stretch for you if you have a deeper relationship with them, the traditional non-bank mortgage Lender really has to make sure to stay within lending guidelines. Your bank may have a portfolio of loans that they have made to keep their depository relationships strong, and they could have the flexibility to help you if the need arises.

Mortgage Brokers

If you would like an alternative to both the bank and the non-bank mortgage Lender, your local mortgage broker could be just what you need. Mortgage brokers are able to place your home loan with any number of different Lenders in an effort to get you the best rates and fees available in the market. Brokers also have access to a wider variety of loan programs than the typical bank or non-bank mortgage Lender, because they are not limited to their "own" products and pricing. As an example: If you were to visit a bank or a non-bank mortgage Lender for a home loan to purchase your dream home, you will have access to all of the loan options that Lender has available to them. If your situation does not fit the guidelines for those loan options, these entities may not have an alternative solution for you. If you are dealing with a mortgage broker, they likely have access to multiple different Lenders with multiple different lending options for you.

Another benefit to having these types of options is that interest rates vary from Lender to Lender. If you are lucky enough to select the exact non-bank mortgage Lender who has the lowest rate on the day you complete your application, you win! If you happen to be with any other Lender who does not happen to be the best on that day, you may pay a higher interest rate than you should, which would mean more expense to you over the life of your loan. Your mortgage broker can work with many different Lenders, providing you with the benefit of not having to shop around yourself. Think of them like a hotel search engine – only for mortgages!

A potential drawback to working with a mortgage broker would be that they are not employed by the Lender making the ultimate decision to approve your home loan. Some Lenders will move heaven and earth to make a loan work if one of their employees has made verbal commitments to you the borrower. They generally might do this to avoid any potential customer service issues caused by their own employees. If your mortgage broker made a commitment that the Lender cannot live up to, you both could be stuck.

On-line versus "brick and mortar" offices

With all of the advertising regarding "Rocket" mortgages today, it should come as no surprise that not all Mortgage Loan Originators live and work in your neighborhood. Sometimes, they work together in a centralized location (or locations) so that they can service customers across multiple time zones. This can be a benefit for both the Lenders they represent and the borrowers they help because information can be shared at times that are convenient for the borrower. And with so much of the mortgage lending business completed electronically today, there really is little need for an actual face-to-face meeting with your Mortgage Loan Originator.

By contrast, most local banks still have a brick and mortar location in or near many major metropolitan cities. This provides an opportunity to stop by and leave paperwork without the need to scan and email the documentation to your mortgage team. I want to be sure to provide a word of advice here. You need to be very cautious when sending any non-public information (NPI) through electronic means. If you must send documentation electronically, be sure the recipient either 1) has a secure portal for you to upload it or 2) can receive password-protected documents to their electronic mailbox. While there is no certain way to stop thieves who want to get their hands on your private information, you can absolutely take steps to ensure as much security as possible on your end.

In most states, mortgage Lenders are not required to have brick and mortar offices in order to conduct business there. As we have seen, the on-line connection can be extremely convenient for you, as the borrower, to communicate with your mortgage team. If you are more comfortable meeting face-to-face with your mortgage expert, then you will need to seek out a local brick and mortar office at your local bank, a non-bank mortgage Lender or a local mortgage broker.

Do your own homework!

While much has been written about the mortgage process, there simply is no substitute for making sure that you are an educated consumer. You've taken a great first step by choosing to read this material, but there is so much information surrounding this process that we simply cannot cover it all in this short book. Much of what we have discussed here just scratches the surface of the amount of information available, and it can be tempting to just move ahead without truly doing your own homework. Yes, I have over 25 years of experience in mortgage lending, and yes, I believe I can provide you with some valuable information that will help you become better informed. But the final decision is up to you.

The great news is that the Internet provides a limitless source of information on every topic you can dream up. Use it! Use your social media circles of influence. Check out company reviews, and even interview multiple mortgage providers before you make the final decision to use one of them for your mortgage needs. I've mentioned to others before; ultimately, to hire a mortgage person to work for you means you need to feel comfortable that they are working in your best interest. Really, the only way to get to this level of comfort is to speak with them on the telephone, meet with them in person or at least obtain a reference from someone you know and trust already. Be informed – Knowledge is Power!

ABOUT THE AUTHOR

Jon is a seasoned Real Estate Finance executive with over 25 years of direct leadership experience over all mortgage banking functions. He has an expert-level understanding of Sales, Operations, Capital Markets and Servicing. Jon currently serves as President / CEO of JW Mortgage Group, LLC, an independent mortgage broker based in Central Florida serving the residential real estate financing needs of all Floridians.